BEN FRANKLIN'S

GUIDE TO WEALTH

BEN FRANKLIN'S

GUIDE TO WEALTH

BEING A 21ST CENTURY TREATISE
ON WHAT IT TAKES
TO LIVE A THRIFTY LIFE

ERIN BARRETT AND JACK MINGO

CONARI PRESS

Conari Press
An imprint of Turner Publishing Company
www.turnerpublishing.com

Library of Congress Cataloging-in-Publication Data

Mingo, Jack,

    Ben Franklin's guide to wealth : being a 21st century treatise on what it takes to live a thrifty life / Jack Mingo and Erin Barrett.

        p. cm.

    Includes bibliographical references and index.

    ISBN 1-57324-953-X (pbk.)

    1. Finance, Personal. 2. Time management. 3. Wealth. 4. Saving and investment. 5. Conduct of life. 6. Franklin, Benjamin, 1706-1790. Way to wealth. I. Barrett, Erin. II. Title.

    HG179.M525 2004

    332.024--dc22

                            2004008810

Typeset in Minion by Grace Peirce

Printed in the United States of America

10 9 8 7 6 5 4 3 2

CONTENTS

INTRODUCTION

What Can Ben Franklin Teach Us?

A word to the wise is enough. —*Ben Franklin*

Most people live dysfunctional financial lives. As a result, many people are miserable. The misery comes in many packages: pressing credit card bills, the disaster of lost income, fear of the future, or getting stuck in dead-end jobs because they "can't afford" to leave.

There is plenty of miracle money advice out there. Most seems designed to add even more stress and fear. Do you need an extra job? Have you bought a house yet? Do you have a huge stock portfolio? Are you as rich as your neighbors? Have you saved up the hundreds of thousands of dollars you'll need to get your kids in the "right" schools or the millions of dollars you'll need to retire "comfortably"?

But perhaps the modern cures are wrong. If you're someone who has followed the financial "wisdom" of the last few decades, you may have seen your pension disappear as a result of corporate corruption or your stock investments die in the dot-com bust, or you may have suffered unemployment or the squeeze of enforced overtime as jobs disappeared and tax breaks went to the obscenely rich. The "new" ideas have been shown to be wanting. So where do we look? Perhaps we should listen to the advice of the guy who appears on the $100 bill: Ben Franklin. While thought of as hopelessly outmoded in this orgy of modern-day borrowing and investment, maybe old-fashioned, "penny-saved-is-a-penny-earned" Ben had it right all along.

They that won't be counseled, can't be helped.
—Ben Franklin

Benjamin Franklin was absolutely brilliant in many areas of life. And he wasn't a "do as I say, not as I do" sort of guy. He actually applied his ideas to the circumstances in his own life. He compiled his thoughts about how to live a healthy financial life, and he followed them and became wealthy. How wealthy? Rich enough to have a full life, to travel extensively, to follow his intellectual musings, and to help him become the most accomplished scientist, inventor, political agitator, diplomat, writer, and journalist of his time. When he died, Franklin left a fortune, both in money and in his legacy to the world.

When you consider the scope of his accomplishments, they seem even more impressive when you consider that the only advantages Franklin had were intelligence, curiosity, native good sense, and a home life that gave him a proclivity for hard work and thrift. He was the fifteenth child of seventeen, the youngest son of Josiah and Abiah Franklin. His father supported his family by making soap and candles in Boston.

Benjamin Franklin received only two years of formal schooling. He got good grades in reading, fair grades in writing, and poor grades in mathematics. At the age of ten, his father decided the family could afford no more education for him and brought him home to work in the family business, melting tallow and cutting wicks. In his teen years, he was apprenticed to an older brother, who owned a print shop, but at age seventeen he ran away from his commitment to Philadelphia. There he worked for several printers until, at age twenty-four, he opened his own print shop and began writing and printing the *Philadelphia Gazette*.

> *Experience keeps a dear school, but fools will learn in no other, and scarce in that.*

Believing that "leisure is the time for doing something useful" and that "the doors of wisdom are never shut," Franklin read everything he could get his hands on, worked systematically on his writing and math, and studied French, German, Italian, Spanish, and Latin, making himself one of the best-educated people of his time.

Meanwhile, his printing business prospered. One of his neighbors noted at the time:

> The industry of that Franklin is superior to anything I ever saw. . . . I see him still at work when I go home from the club; and he is at work again before his neighbors are out of bed.

The *Gazette* became one of the most successful papers in the colonies at that time, but Franklin achieved his biggest success with *Poor Richard's Almanack*, which he published annually under the name "Richard Saunders" from 1733 until 1758. The essay that has been reprinted since then as "The Way to Wealth" (see appendix) appeared in the last issue of the *Almanack*, and included quotes from the previous two and a half decades, humorously framed by a self-mocking tall tale. It is upon these aphorisms that this book is based.

Sometimes a particular book changes its authors' lives. When we began writing this one, we decided that if we followed Franklin's advice and example, we might end up just as fortunate as he was. Frankly, we had a lot to learn and still do. Although Mr. Franklin's advice may seem severe and old fashioned, we discovered that we got a great deal of satisfaction—and improved our financial situation—trying to live the lessons herein. We hope you will, too.

There are ten main sections to the book. You can go through them in order or skip around based on your needs. Read one a day or one a week. We encourage you to use this guide creatively in a way that will benefit you the most.

Good luck and best wishes for a happy, prosperous life.

Erin Barrett
Jack Mingo

> *If you will not hear reason, she'll surely rap your knuckles.—Ben Franklin*

TIME IS MONEY

*Doest thou love life? Then do not squander
time, for that is the stuff life is made of.*

How do you spend your time? Despite the cliché, time is not *really* money. However, in some ways it helps to think of it as being very much *like* money: You can spend it wisely or foolishly. You have a finite amount of it. And it's likely to slip away unnoticed if you're not careful.

Are you getting the best value from your time? Just as many goods are not worth the money spent on them, many daily activities are not worth the time spent on them. While some may decide that a single-minded pursuit of money is the best use of their time, others will want to invest their time in other ways that they find valuable. To become aware of how you invest your time (or simply let it slip away), experiment with keeping a time and activity log.

Try this exercise: Keep a log in quarter-hour increments to see what you spend your time on during a typical week. At the end of the week, categorize your time spent and add up the total amount of time for each category. How much time do you spend commuting, attending meetings, or doing errands? How much time do you spend watching television, talking on the phone, or surfing the Internet? How much time do you spend feeding your mind, sleeping, developing your talents, organizing, cleaning, preparing meals, or engaged in worthwhile activities with loved ones?

Most people are shocked and chagrined to see many hours they spend on certain unproductive activities, and how little they spend on ones that improve themselves, their financial lives, and their connections with the people they love. Using a time log may help you see how certain times of the day are consistently productive while others are times when you are most likely to get distracted and be unproductive.

Once you've got a clear list of your week's activities, take a good look at your log. Draw three columns next to your entries. In the first column, number the activity from

1 to 10 to reflect how much or little that activity adds to meeting your financial goals. In the second column, put a number that reflects how much or little pleasure that activity adds to your life. Then compare the two columns. In an ideal life, the activities that support your financial goals would also be ones that give you pleasure. At the very least, your time expenditure should have some kind of balance between things you love and things you do to increase your financial freedom.

Finally, in your third column, keeping in mind what you've put in the first two columns, put a plus sign next to things you'd like to invest more time on, and a minus sign next to the things you'd like to spend less time on.

Have you inventoried a week's activities in your time log and found that little looks like something you want to put time into? Are you feeling "lazy" and incapable of spending your time usefully? Have you found that you don't "love life"? If so, then it's time for some self-reflection.

Are you burned out by your job? Finding your hobbies and home responsibilities less than satisfying? Feeling far removed from your dreams? Experiencing alienation in your relationships with people? If so, consider getting checked out by a doctor, physically and psychologically. Common physical conditions (for example, depression or hypothyroidism) can drag you down and make you feel tired and despondent. Drug or alcohol abuse can manifest itself in a variety of sneakily debilitating ways. Perhaps you need to talk with a counselor about some longstanding issues with your work, relationships, sense of helplessness, and so on.

What we want to tell you is that it isn't hopeless. It is possible to change your life, do much of what you want to do, and stop doing much of what you don't want to do. Yes, you may have to take some risks, take a leap, be willing to balance the security of inertia against the risks of making changes. But it's worth thinking about, clarifying, planning, preparing, and recruiting your friends, allies, and loved ones to offer support.

Leisure is time for doing something useful;
this leisure the diligent man will obtain, but
the lazy man never; so that a life of leisure
and a life of laziness are two things.

Dare we say it? Doing work for yourself is not only good for your pocketbook, but it's good for your soul as well. True, you can pay somebody to prepare your food (either directly or indirectly by using convenience foods). You can pay somebody to do your yard chores, your cleaning, your car maintenance, and so on. You can pay somebody to prepare your taxes, carry your bags, paint and decorate your home, and do the work at your place of business. You can even pay somebody to raise your children, educate them, and teach them how to play sports.

You *can* do that, and sometimes it makes sense to do so, but let us suggest that, whenever you can, it's best to do it yourself.

You might add up the money you make per hour and compare it with the money you'd spend per hour on an outside worker and decide that since you make more money per hour than a yard worker, you'd be better off working the extra hours at your own job, hiring a lower-paid worker, and pocketing the difference.

This might be a completely rational decision. However, it also may be a false economy. For example, if your work is one where you sit all day, working outside in the yard pushing a mower (preferably manual, not a gas guzzler) will be great for your health and may save you the cost of a health club membership (or a triple bypass). If your job is complicated and filled with stress, you may find meditative solace in painting, digging, sewing patches on jeans, washing dishes, organizing drawers, or building shelves. And kids? No matter what other jobs you have, you may find that genuinely connecting with kids can be the most rewarding of all.

Frankly, most people have to have down time from their normal labors. What you do with that downtime—use it or waste it—is the difference between leisure and laziness.

Plough deep, while sluggards sleep, and
you shall have corn to sell and to keep.

How much of your budget do you spend on food? For most Americans food is the third biggest item, taking up about 14 percent of their total income.

Consider becoming a "weekend farmer"—a vegetable gardener. During World War II, Victory Gardens were all the rage. To support the war effort, the government sent out booklets with instructions on how every family could start their own vegetable and herb garden. The campaign took off, and families everywhere were putting their own homegrown vegetables on their dinner tables. It may seem like a lot of work if you've never tried, but it can save you money at the market. How much money? With two-fifths of an acre, a family of four can grow 75 percent of their food, saving $3,000 a year.

But maybe you don't have that much land available. Or worse, you live in an apartment, and have only a patio or balcony. While it's true that you won't be able to produce as much as someone who has a huge backyard, you can still plant your potatoes, squash, tomatoes, peas, beans, peppers, and herbs in pots and bins, on your patio or in a sunny window.

Regardless of the size of their "back forty"—whether forty acres, forty feet square, or forty plants in pots—most people get a great deal of pleasure out of growing at least some of their own food. You may find that you do too.

Employ thy time well,
if thou meanest to gain leisure.

It's one thing to want to work hard for something. However, if you're always busy, if you're always working long hours and feeling dragged down by it, it may be time to reassess some things.

Songwriter Ray Davies once asked that if life is for living, what is living for? One thing we know is that all work and no play is not the goal of living. So what's the problem?

- Perhaps you're not organized enough in your work. If you could procrastinate less and could do more work in less time, you'd have more time left over in the day.

- Perhaps you could use time that normally is dead time. Are you using your commute time wisely? Get out of your car if you can and bicycle for the exercise, for example. Or use carpooling and public transportation so you can use the time for something more productive than driving through rush hour. What about lunch time? Don't just sit at a table in a lunchroom or a restaurant—take a walk and clear your head, take a short nap or meditation break, or read something while you eat.

- Perhaps you need to prioritize your work and give more of your time to finish the activities that are most important. Let other tasks slide, if necessary.

- Perhaps you need an attitude change about your job. Perhaps you're overvaluing it, avoiding it, or living in fear about losing your job and letting yourself be taken advantage of.

- Or, perhaps you need to consider whether you'd be happier in another career, and if so, start making plans to pursue it.

If time be of all things the most precious, wasting time must be the greatest prodigality, since lost time is never found again.

What uses up your time without giving much of anything back? Think about turning it all off—the television, computer games, the Internet, the sports obsessions, even the friends and family members who drain your time and energy without nourishing you in return. Life's too short. What would it be like to ruthlessly take your life back so you can fall in love with it again? What would it be like to value your time as the precious thing it is?

How much more than is necessary do we spend in sleep, forgetting that the sleeping fox catches no poultry, and that there will be sleeping enough in the grave.

Sleep less? To many people, that seems like difficult advice to follow—they already feel sleep deprived. But Ben isn't really advocating less sleep than is healthy. After all, he's famous for coining the phrase, "Early to bed and early to rise, makes a man healthy, wealthy, and wise." The problem is not completely the issue of when you go to bed and when you wake up, but what you do at night when you're awake. In Franklin's time, staying up late meant wastefully burning expensive candles instead of using the light from the sun. (In fact, Franklin successfully promoted Daylight Saving Time in the United States as a way of saving candles.) It also often meant "wine, women, and song," none of which were necessarily conducive to productive use of time. In our time, the fact that we don't go to sleep when we're tired, but instead stay up and find modern-day amusements, means that we have an awful lot of people who are sleep-deprived. Which, of course, makes it awfully hard to do your best during daylight.

ෘ

He that riseth late must trot all day, and
shall scarce overtake his business at night.

This is the crux of Franklin's philosophy of getting up with the sun, using time productively, and then getting well-deserved rest. It's a system that still works—getting to bed early instead of dallying with "wine and women," or modern day distractions of television and the Internet.

ෘ

What we call time enough, always proves
little enough. Let us then be up and be doing,
and doing to the purpose; so by diligence shall
we do more with less perplexity.

Managing your time is a skill that you can learn, no matter how disorganized or prone to procrastination you are. If it's your problem, you've probably already discovered that it's not particularly effective to beat yourself up about it. Instead, take it as something you simply haven't fully learned yet. There are entire books about the subject, but here are some tips to get you started:

- Don't concentrate on how busy you are—concentrate on your results. After all, a frenzy of activity won't get you far if you're trying to shovel gravel with a pitchfork.

- Use a "To Do" list each day to help you prioritize what the most important activities are for the day.

- For each complex goal on your "To Do" list, simplify the tasks by creating an Action Plan, listing the steps you need to do to achieve that goal.

- Next to each entry, put a number from 1 to 5, with the highest priority being 1.

- Redraft your list so that the most important things are first, and the least important are at the bottom. Then do them in order, from most important to least. Anything still left gets put on tomorrow's list.

꙳

Industry pays debts,
while despair increaseth them.

In the face of money woes, it is easy to fall into despair.
But hopelessness is rarely an accurate reflection of reality.
Whatever the condition you find yourself in, there are
aspects of it that could be worse. There is plenty of reason
for hope, and for counting blessings, even in what seem to
be the worst of times.

Not that it's always easy. It's often very difficult to get
moving and do what needs to be done when things look
bleak. But what we want to get across is that difficulty is
not the same as impossibility. When things look dark, it's
the time to get moving and do what has to be done.
What needs doing? Make a list of the steps you need to
do today, and resolve to do half of them by lunchtime.
Stop thinking about it and get to it. Need to find a job?
Get your resume together, get out there, make your phone
calls, send out your letters. You don't need to "feel like it"
to do something—do it anyway!

Don't judge the effort, just do it. Make the activity the
substitute for the worry, self-blame, and hopelessness. Are
you prone to waking up in the middle of the night with
your concerns pressing in on you? When you go to bed,
designate a task for such an occurrence. Set a time limit
for lying in bed worrying—if you're not asleep again in

ten minutes, get up and do the task until you're exhausted enough to sleep again.

*Sloth makes all things
difficult, but industry all easy.*

Okay, having established the importance of using your time wisely, let's talk about equal time. "Productivity" does not necessarily mean letting your work day slop into the time that is your own. Whether you are working for someone else or for yourself, you need to make boundaries that differentiate your work life from your home life. If you are industrious during your work time, make sure you give the same attention to the rest of your life. What's the point of living if you never stop doing your job?

Balance is important. By being as efficient and productive in your free time as you are in your work time, you can get done what you need and want to do and still have time for starting new projects, learning new skills, and setting new goals to keep life interesting. Learn a new way of looking at the world, dream, find a niche somewhere, or take on a personal challenge that is worth your time, especially one that will make or save some money.

SECTION 2

SLOTHFULNESS

ONE HUNDRED DOLLARS

Taxes are indeed very heavy, and if those laid on by the government were the only ones we had to pay, we might more easily discharge them; but we have many others, and much more grievous to some of us. We are taxed twice as much by our idleness, three times as much by our pride, and four times as much by our folly, and from these taxes the commissioners cannot ease or deliver us by allowing an abatement. . . . It would be thought a hard government that should tax its people one-tenth part of their time, to be employed in its service, but idleness taxes many of us much more.

This is a recurring theme from the honorable Mr. Franklin: We can complain about external roadblocks and speed bumps—be they the government, unfortunate circumstances, our bosses, the economy and so on—but in reality external problems are a small part of what is holding us back. Most of our difficulties are in fact self-inflicted, and until we declare our independence and make revolution against our own worst impulses, our excuses and scapegoats will be simply empty fulminations. Furthermore, as Franklin observes, our own laziness, pride, and folly costs us more than we think. If we spent as much energy diminishing these unproductive traits as we do trying to reduce our taxes, we'd be richer indeed.

Sloth, by bringing on diseases,
absolutely shortens life. Sloth, like rust,
consumes faster than labor wears,
while the used key is always bright.

It is true that willful inactivity is bad for body and purse. Get up and get something done, even if you don't feel like it. Having said that, however, we realize that though it's easy to see sloth as mere laziness, there are often deeper reasons why some people live a "slothful" life.

Do you feel like you're firing on three cylinders? Do you just want to rest or veg out in your spare time? It may be a sign that something is terribly wrong. Good hard work that moves you forward in life should be a profoundly satisfying experience. If activity is discouraging and difficult, you might want to look into the reason why. Perhaps you suffer from a physical problem or depression. Perhaps you're in the wrong line of work. Whatever the reason, inactivity will drag you down over time.

A productive person is invariably a happier, healthier person. Whatever you decide to put your energies into, strive to be happy in your labors; not just your primary job, but your other labors as well—the things you do to keep your living space livable, your inner life fulfilled, and you and your loved ones happy and healthy. That is your job as well, and most people fail in these arenas. Ponder this: The average American parent spends nine times more time shopping than they do playing with their kids. We suspect that the average person spends even less time keeping up with the job of staying healthy, in good shape, and rust-free.

જ⁓

Laziness travels so slowly,
that Poverty soon overtakes him.

Laziness can drain your economic well-being in a dozen ways:

- Laziness can make you decide to forgo opportunities for better jobs or promising projects because they seem to be just "too much trouble."

- Laziness can make you prone to get-rich-quick schemes that promise affluence without hard work. Whether it's a hot stock tip, a surefire investment, or a pyramid scheme, "easy" ways to riches are usually not so easy, and are more likely to take your riches than generate them.

- Laziness makes you more likely to drive than walk, eat out rather than cook, hire someone instead of doing your own yard work, and use power tools when elbow grease could do you some good.

- Laziness means looking for shortcuts that bring a short-term advantage rather than providing high quality products or service, which will benefit you more in the end. It means giving short shrift to details and other hallmarks of good quality.

MINDING YOUR BUSINESS

Drive thy business, let not that drive thee.

What's the best way to accomplish your goal of living within your means and saving toward things you want? It's largely a matter of attitude.

You can try to live without want by working toward becoming so rich that you'll be able to afford everything you'll ever desire. Or you can live richly by saving a modest amount for emergencies and working toward managing your urges and reducing your wants. A very few people will achieve the first state, although it is questionable whether it could ever really be possible to become rich enough to satisfy any conceivable whim. But almost anybody can achieve the second if they work at it. As Henry David Thoreau said, "A man is rich in proportion to the things he can afford to let alone."

In making changes to reduce your expenses by reducing your wants, a money program is similar to a diet and exercise program. If you look at a diet and concentrate on all the stuff you're going to have to give up, you're pretty much guaranteed to fail. However, if you look on it as an adventure, as something that will help you feel better and live a longer, thinner, healthier, more active life, then it's easier to concentrate on what you're getting instead of what you're giving up.

With a money program, it often works best to change your life dramatically and boldly. Make the new way of living a hobby, even a mild obsession, until it eventually becomes an automatic response. Don't mope about the things you're giving up; instead, celebrate the day-to-day successes. Give yourself a pat on the back every time you resist falling into old patterns.

Find measurable yardsticks to compare your results with those of your old, profligate ways: How much have you paid down your debts since last month? How much money do you have in savings compared to this time last month and last year? How close are you to your intermediate goals and your long-term goals?

Cheer your successes, and analyze (and then forgive) your failures. Find some inexpensive ways to reward yourself when you've done well—exchange a backrub with a friend or loved one, take a bike ride or a walk, or take a long, relaxing bubble bath. Remind yourself what a great job you're doing. You deserve it.

What signifies wishing and hoping for better times? We may make these times better if we bestir ourselves.

Don't wait around for miracles to happen, and money to fill your coffers. Take matters into your own hands. If you haven't already set some financial goals, do so. Do you want to purchase a home? A car? A vacation to China? Perhaps it's something more practical like needing to insulate your home, make room for a new member of the family, or fix a leaky roof. Figure out some concrete objectives now. If you can't come up with any at the moment, reserve the right to think about it, but move on to the next step anyway.

Once you're aware of how much you're making each month and how much you're spending, you're in a good position to begin saving. Start by picking an amount you're going to set aside: even 5 percent or 10 percent is better than most people's 0 percent. Many good money managers suggest putting away enough to force you to live completely within your budget—and perhaps do without some of the non-necessities you enjoy—but don't make things dire for yourself. It's important as you budget and save that you learn to control your money, and not let your money control you. That includes making sure you don't completely deprive yourself while trying to reach your financial goals.

Industry need not wish.

What can you do to increase your income? First of all, let's talk about what *not* to do.

- Don't fall for scams, pyramid schemes (Amway, etc.), or other get-rich plans that will more likely drain money from your pockets than add it.

- Don't do anything that you consider to be immoral. When he was a struggling printer, Ben Franklin was offered a generous amount of money to print something he considered scandalous and libelous. He wrote: "To determine whether I should publish it or not, I went home in the evening, purchased a twopenny loaf at the baker's, and with the water from the pump made my supper; I then wrapped myself up in my great-coat, and laid down on the floor and slept until morning, when, on another loaf and a mug of water, I made my breakfast. From this regimen, I felt no inconvenience whatever. Finding I can live in this manner, I have formed a determination never to prostitute my press to the purposes of corruption and abuse of this kind."

What is more likely to increase your earnings?

- Can you make more money by working more or better at the job you're already doing?

- If not, how much free time can you find to work a second job?

- Is there anything you can do at home with (or at least near) your family that will generate money?

- Are there any hobbies, interests, or longtime skills that you and your family can use to generate money—either directly, or indirectly by advising others or teaching them the skills you already have? For example, teaching writing, art, or music is often more lucrative than writing,

painting, or playing. Many people would love
to learn basic car maintenance and repair,
carpentry, home repairs, knitting, or any number
of skills that you may have to offer.

*He that hath a trade hath an estate, and he
that hath a calling hath an office of profit and
honor; but then the trade must be worked at,
and calling followed, or neither the estate, nor
the office, will enable us to pay our taxes.*

How many people hate their jobs? Is it any surprise that
more heart attacks occur between 8:00 and 9:00 Monday
morning than any other time of the week?

Maybe it's hard to think of your job as a trade. A
blacksmith or a shoemaker in Franklin's time, for
example, could measure personal performance by quality
of products, speed of work, amount of work, and money
coming in. One of the problems of the modern world
is that many of us work in large corporations where
there is little chance for pride or direct feedback on our
performance, our "trade," and for many there's a sense
that work occurs in a meaningless vacuum.

Ben Franklin offers the sound advice that we strive to
make our working lives both a "trade" and a "calling."
Without a sense of purpose, honor, pride, and direct profit

from our efforts, our work diminishes and constricts us. Too many people end up with hopes, dreams, and brains lying dormant. They live their lives waiting for the years to tick by until they retire. Sadly, the ones who give up so much in life for the security of a job become the ones with the least job security, since they are often the most expendable when the company decides it needs to shed jobs.

What's the alternative? One is to work to find meaning and pride in the job you are doing. Another is to find a different profession, one that gives both a sense of craft and calling. Why both? Because how you feel about what you do will fluctuate. Being skillful gives you something to be proud of, even when you're feeling a lack of inspiration. And inspiration keeps you going, even when you hit setbacks and plateaus in your craft. You may find it surprising, but the question "What do you want to be when you grow up?" is as pertinent now as it was when you were a kid.

By diligence and patience
the mouse ate in two the cable.

We all have our weaknesses. Many of us are habitual spenders. Perhaps money was tightly controlled in our childhood homes, and, so, as adults we rebel and spend without thought. When we're feeling low, or something goes badly at work or home, breaking the budget and buying something may give us a rush that staves off the negative feelings.

Others of us won't spend anything at all. We save, save, and save. Perhaps it's an inborn trait. Did you hoard your Halloween or Christmas candy for months, only divvying out a piece at a time—or maybe none at all? Maybe you were raised with no money, and the risk associated with spending money now seems terribly frightening. After all, if we make purchases or investments, we are taking some risk. What if we lose our jobs the next day and suddenly can't pay our bills? What if we default on our mortgage? We could end up with nothing, out on the street, sharing a cardboard box with five guys named Mack.

These are extremes, but the way in which we see our wealth can be heavily distorted by our feelings. Irrational behavior of either extreme, be it excessive spending or compulsive saving, is not the way to taking control of our finances.

To start changing your relationship to money, first you have to think and reflect. Look at the feelings you have when you spend money on something. Recovering alcoholics sometimes have to stay away from bars and friends who like to drink in order to stay sober, especially during times of negative emotions. Similarly, shopaholics who compulsively spend to ease negative emotions like rejection, sadness, and fear must learn to stay away from shopping opportunities, particularly at those times when they experience disappointments and other "triggers."

Before you take control of your money and figure out where it's going each month, it would be good to monitor your own psychology and figure out if irrational emotions are contributing to problems with your finances. Then start making small, doable changes every month to move closer to your goals. If you're a spender, start putting away some amount of money from every paycheck. If you're a compulsive saver, make a small, unnecessary purchase or two once in awhile. It's not easy, but taking the time to do so will help you diligently gnaw through the cord that binds you to your bad money habits.

ﮩﮩﮩﮩ

Little strokes fell great oaks.

This saying from Ben Franklin can be seen as a guideline for tackling large problems and as a caution to take care of even the seemingly small things so they don't create larger problems.

As the saying shows, you can accomplish anything if you break the task at hand into small parts. You are not going to fell a mighty tree with one ax swing, but you can with a few hundred ax swings. It may take time to change your relationship to finances, but if you work at it you will succeed. The warning also applies well to financial health. A mighty wind or a single lightning strike may knock over an oak, but, similarly, hundreds of small expenses can topple the tree of your financial stability and well being.

He that by the plough would thrive,
himself must either hold or drive.

Investing in a business or stock is not something to do with money you need. As many would-be investors have learned the hard way: If you can't afford to lose it, don't invest it.

One way to increase your chances in investments is to put your money in businesses you understand. It's way too risky to invest in a company that makes something for a market that you don't have the expertise to evaluate. If you can't understand the product or the market, you become susceptible to and dependent on the advice of others. Far better to invest in beer companies if that's an industry you honestly know about than in high-tech companies that make gadgets about which you don't have a clue.

Stock genius Warren Buffett once suggested that you should know about a company and feel good about its products and future—that if you wouldn't feel good about owning its stock for ten years, then you shouldn't own it for ten minutes.

⤞⤝

God helps them that help themselves.

This is one of Ben Franklin's sayings that has been repeated so many times and become such a cliché that people have stopped thinking about what it really means.

Ironically, many people like to quote it as a reason to do nothing for the poor. (In fact, many people who quote it seem to think that it came from the Bible.) That's a total distortion of what our wise friend Ben is trying to say here. He was a strong believer in giving generously to charity (see page 106). What he's suggesting is not to judge others, but to hold ourselves up to the highest standard of behavior.

The message, of course, is that the best way to make a miracle happen is to get off your knees and get on your feet. Stop praying for divine intervention and get busy. Let us suggest from experience the best way to make Ben Franklin's program work for you: Catch the spirit of what he has to say and put some real thought into how it relates to your own financial situation and goals. Visualize making radical changes in the areas where your financial lifeblood is bleeding away. Once you see that real change is possible, even desirable, make a single-minded commitment to implementing the steps to lead you to your goal.

Feel good about the changes. Don't see them as giving up something, but as you would if you were finally achieving health after years of being bedridden. Celebrate your victories, enjoy the heady ones: cutting up your credit cards, canceling your unneeded expenses, and watching your savings grow week by week.

Keep the shop, and thy shop will keep thee.

Let's say you've got a small business that is doing well. In fact, it's doing better than you can keep up with. What's the best way to handle your success? Become more selective in the work you take on? Raise your prices to reduce your workload while increasing your profit margin? Or expand your capacity and your work force?

This paradoxical dilemma is one that successful business people have to deal with. There is no single right answer to this. The answer that works best will depend on many factors. It requires foresight and flexibility, creativity and being straightforward about the facts of your business. It often requires discussion and brainstorming. The success of many businesses also often rests on whether the individual or individuals who are responsible for the key decisions and strategy can learn to share responsibility and decision- making as the business grows and evolves.

This can be harder than you might imagine for the founders of most small businesses. The skills of creating a business are much different than those needed to expand and manage a business. Many founders and innovators fail dramatically at it. Many of them, if their business grows, find (or sometimes their shareholders decide) that they need to be banished upstairs to a higher level of management where they can't harm the day-to-day workings of the growing business. The history of many businesses includes dramatic moments when it becomes clear that the founder is incapable of managing what the business has become.

A key to good management is knowing your abilities and your limitations. True, skillful people management can be learned, but it's also true that most people are best at a particular management level. If you're a hands-on person, you'll likely become frustrated if your job changes to one of meetings, paperwork, and managing others. In that case, you may want to keep your business small enough to be manageable, or get out of the way and let somebody else manage. Or sell it outright, and start a new venture.

SECTION 4

ATTENTION TO DETAIL

ONE HUNDRED DOLLARS

*Work while it is called today, for you
know not how much you may be
hindered tomorrow.*

When do you do your best work? When are
you inspired? When in the top of health
and feeling energetic? How do you do when
you're excited by what you're doing?

All these things make productivity easier, and should be
welcomed whenever they appear. However, the sign of a
true professional is someone who can do good work even
at a bad time, even when feeling lousy and uninspired.

It is easy, especially in creative professions, to wait
around until inspiration hits, until everything feels lined

up and in place. There are many people who claim that
they can't do their work until they've done little rituals,
eaten the right foods, drunk a coffee or a beer, had a
smoke, turned off the phone, put the kids to bed, or any
other "preparatory ritual."

Whatever the reason or intent, setting any sort of
prerequisite conditions means that you won't get work
done that you could have. If you have a chance to work
now, do it. Don't put off work, because you might feel
even lousier and less inspired tomorrow. Robert Louis
Stevenson wrote his 60,000-word classic *Dr. Jekyll &*
Mr. Hyde in six days while deathly ill with tuberculosis.
Don't wait, don't hope for the muses to inspire you—do
whatever you need to do—today.

If you were a servant, would you not be
ashamed that a good master should catch
you idle? Are you then your own master, be
ashamed to catch yourself idle.

Learning how to be our own masters is one of the big
challenges, because we are taught from an early age to be
servants.

Here's what we mean. As children, we learn to follow
the dictates of our parents and our teachers. We also learn

to slack off when they're not looking and look busy when they are. The problem, of course, is that part of growing up is to mature so that you manage yourself and your time. You become your own boss, often literally (as in starting your own business) or at least figuratively (in the sense of taking control of your own life and time). Managing other people is an art; managing yourself is at least as hard. What kind of a boss are you to yourself? And what kind of subordinate?

Do you imagine that sloth will afford
you more comfort than labor? Trouble
springs from idleness, and grievous
toil from needless ease.

Most of us are drowning under modern "labor-saving devices." To begin with, there's the expense of purchasing these gadgets. Then there's the expense of storing them and powering them. And finally, there's the "time-saving" illusion. For example, consider a leaf blower versus a rake—it's expensive to buy and run, it pollutes, and the time it saves is often negligible. Meanwhile, the noise annoys everybody around you, and destroys any chance for you to have a quiet thought while working outdoors.

You've got to wonder especially about the addiction we have to the "granddaddy" of labor-saving devices, the car.

For most people it's the largest single expense after their house. Can we really afford this and does it really save us time? Your average car trip covers a distance of only a few miles. These short distances are perfect for bicycling, jogging, or even walking. In fact, given the time it takes to park and the delays from traffic congestion, most bicyclists can match the speed of cars, within minutes, on a trip to the local store.

What are all these "labor-saving devices" costing you? Money? Life-saving and life-enhancing exercise? Does the time you "save" make up for what you lose?

Fly pleasures, and they'll follow you.

The founder of Baskin-Robbins had a father who made him work in the family store. He was told, "Work now while your friends play, and later you'll play while your friends work." The idea is that working now to make your fortune secure is a good way to give you flexibility in the future to do what you want. If you seek pleasure above all else now, you will find that the joy you experience is fleeting. Instead, if you shift your goal toward doing meaningful things with your time, you'll find unexpected, lasting pleasures.

Find ways to make everything you do in your life support and nourish your own growth and development.

"Let your food be your medicine and your medicine be your food," advised Hippocrates a few thousand years ago. In a similar vein, let your productiveness give you pleasure and your pleasures be productive.

Want of care does us more damage
than want of knowledge.

Learning to find what's new and interesting in something you've been doing for years is what separates the professional from the dilettante. Find the joy in doing a good job. Find the satisfaction that comes from taking care of your resources or tools. Feel the excitement of discovering new approaches to old problems, of inventing and innovating. The difference between just doing a job and making a career is in your attention to the details.

For want of a nail the shoe was lost; for
want of a shoe the horse was lost, and for
want of a horse the rider was lost, being
overtaken and slain by the enemy; all for
want of care about a horseshoe nail.

It's not just the big things—it's more likely the small things that will end up costing you money and damaging your financial health. This is true in all areas of life, but let's take one example: our modern-day, gas-guzzling "horses." How regularly do most of us do the maintenance that keeps our cars running in good order? As any good mechanic will tell you, it's a false economy to neglect the small stuff and preventative care.

- Oil changes and tune-ups are inexpensive compared to the cost of fixing or replacing your engine. Doing them on schedule can keep your engine purring happily for hundreds of thousands of miles. Keeping your tires at the right inflation level takes just a few minutes once a month and will save you money by increasing tire life and decreasing your gas consumption. And maybe even more importantly, it will help prevent disastrous accidents.

- The importance of preventative maintenance holds equally in your home. Do you check the filters on your furnace and air conditioning in a timely manner? Changing or cleaning them regularly will save you money. Have you fixed your leaky faucets, running toilets, holes and under-insulated spots in your home that let the heat out in winter? If you put attention in these areas, according to an energy study, the average family could reduce energy consumption 30-40 percent while increasing comfort levels. For some families, that means saving an estimated $400-$800 a year.

A little neglect may breed great mischief.

Are you doing the small things to keep yourself healthy? Eliminating fatty foods from your diet? Exercising? Cutting out smoking and excessive drinking? If you won't do it for yourself or your children, do it for your bankbook. Staying healthy will save you a bundle. On the simplest level, when you stay fit you can do your own chores. In addition to saving you unnecessary physical discomfort, staying fit can save you an average of more than $400,000 in medical costs over the course of your life. One study found that sedentary people need assisted living ten to twenty years sooner than those who exercise. Nursing homes cost $40,000-$75,000 a year—do the math.

As our friend Ben would say, penny-pinching on the small stuff that keeps the big stuff running is a classic case of "penny wise and pound foolish."

NOT TRUSTING TOO MUCH

*With our industry, we must likewise be
steady, settled and careful, and oversee
our own affairs with our own eyes, and
not trust too much to others.*

There's a responsible way to trust others and institutions with your financial matters. As Franklin cautions us, we need to take responsibility ourselves and use our healthy discriminative faculties. For example, no matter how much banks and businesses advertise their friendliness and trustworthiness, exercise healthy caution before extending undue trust. Banks and businesses have their own motivations for projecting a certain image of themselves. Often these motivations serve their own financial gain rather than yours. There are dozens of examples of this. The following one is common and can show you how easy it is to not notice hidden fees that are tacked on to a "free" offer.

Most banks offer a savings account that's connected to your main checking account, free of charge. If you overspend your checking account, the bank automatically shifts funds from your savings account to cover the overdraft. This is often touted as a "service" the bank offers, and it sounds like a no-brainer benefit. But looking closer at this particular "service," you may find, as we have, that it's better to do without it.

By automatically protecting you from bouncing checks, it encourages you to not watch your account balance very closely. Not a bad deal for the bank, which would rather you not question why you're paying esoteric fees that are often buried in the bank policy's fine print. For example, by going through our statement we discovered that we were being charged fifty cents every time we used our ATM at a particular store we frequented. We were also charged a hefty fee every time our checking account dipped below a certain balance (the automatic overdraft didn't kick in to prevent this from happening.) Our "free" checking required that we buy checks from the bank at a huge markup. Our bank charged each time we visited non-bank ATMs, which cost us dozens of dollars a month.

Another reason to avoid overdraft protection is that it encourages irresponsible spending. Overdrawing your main account (or any account, for that matter) is a big financial no-no. It means you're not on top of your finances. If getting charged an exorbitant overdraft fee a few times is what it takes to get you back in control of your checkbook totals, consider it an inexpensive education.

Finally, though, there is the most pressing reason not to link your savings with your checking: you might lose it all to freelance thieves (as opposed to the ones who make policy at banks).

You're probably aware of the growing problem of identity theft: If someone gets hold of your name and debit card number, they can drain your checking account and then continue to drain your savings account as well. Unlike credit cards, where you are liable by law for only $50 or $100, you have a very short amount of time to report the theft of your ATM card before you could lose the whole amount.

Savings accounts are important for financial health. They serve as a convenient place to deposit cash for both long- and short-term financial goals. They offer an easy access emergency fund "just in case." Just make sure

they're separate from your checking account. Make sure
that your savings are secure.

> *Trusting too much to others' care is the ruin*
> *of many; for in the affairs of this world men*
> *are saved not by faith, but by the want of it;*
> *but a man's own care is profitable.*

Trust all those smiling people who want to sell you
something? Not on your life. Get it in writing, read
carefully, make sure you know what all those phrases
mean, and make sure what you're really agreeing to is the
same as what you think you're agreeing to.

Caveat emptor ("let the buyer beware") is the watchword
of the day. One would hope that reputable businesses
would work to get your business by keeping things simple,
by providing clear contracts, and by offering decent
services at a reasonable price. But as Franklin cautions us,
smart buyers don't assume anything without verifying for
certain.

> *Not to oversee workmen is to*
> *leave them your purse open.*

Once there was a time when the management of a reputable business would feel shame at using trickery to fleece their best customers. Too often now, though, it's considered the smart way to do business.

For example, the phone company used to provide telephones, upkeep, and reliable service for a reasonable price. Once the industry was opened up and competitive companies began offering phone services, it seems like these companies spend all their best resources trying to figure out how to make sure you misstep into some expensive mistake. Did you think your calling plan would cover international service? Wrong! That's why you're being charged three dollars a minute instead of the advertised ten cents. It's all in the fine print.

Banks, too. It used to be that they were happy to be stodgy, honest, but reasonably profitable places where you'd save your money, keep a checking account, and go to for a major loan. Nowadays, though, they work hard to hide their surcharges, hoping to trick you into calling their info lines one too many times in a month, or visiting their tellers when you have a "limited teller" account, so they can charge you a hefty fee. Worse, they seem happy to ensnare you into charge cards you can't afford, and applaud excitedly if you exceed your balance on your checking account. Because likely you have a clause in the fine print you didn't read that allows them to charge exorbitant fees. In fact, many credit card banks with halfway reasonable rates rely on the fact that most customers will be late making a payment once, because their agreements say that if you're late even one day because the mail was slow, they can automatically raise your credit card interest rate from, say, 16 percent to 28 percent or higher.

Unfortunately, you can run into the same callous business rules with any major purchase like a car or house, cell phone plan, Internet service, home or business loan. If you work for yourself, you'll likely have to issue contracts or sign other people's. Beware of the latter. If you're providing the letter of agreement yourself, remember that return business is important, and that the business that lives by the unfair agreement will likely die from it as well. Strive to create fair, understandable contracts and demand the same from those you do business with. Ultimately, dishonest businesses won't prosper.

THRIFT THROUGH RIGHT EFFORT

He that lives upon hopes will die fasting.
There are no gains without pains.

Deciding to save is the first step, but it takes effort to watch a dream grow. We suggest a couple of practical tips on how to work at building your savings:

- Put aside enough so that you are somewhat squeezed and have to budget. If you've got it available, you'll likely spend it.

- If you use any of your savings for non-goal expenses, consider it a loan. Make sure you're going to be able to pay it back soon so you don't sabotage yourself.

- See if your employer can deposit some of your salary directly into your savings. Many companies offer this service—talk to the payroll office at your business. It's much easier to save it if the money goes automatically into your savings account and doesn't pass through your hands.

- Put most or all of any money you receive over and above your normal income—whether it's outside earnings, a gift, or a bonus—into your savings. Pretending you never got it so it can go directly to the fund you set up will help you achieve your goals.

Handle your tools without mittens; remember that the cat in gloves catches no mice.

Working "hands-on" was important even in Franklin's time. If you want to have control of your money, it helps if you take it into your own hands. Make sure you know where it's going.

"Well, duh!" you say. But you'd be surprised at how many people have only a vague clue of where all the dollars they earn go.

If you're trying to save money for the things you think are important—vacations, investments, food, rent, etc.—you'll want to take a cold clear look at how your money steadily leaks out of your wallet and bank account. Start with this: for a month, keep a diary of every cent you spend. Yes, it sounds burdensome. But here's why it's worth the effort: it makes every spending decision a conscious one. Keeping track of your daily expenses will give you an accurate snapshot of your average month's spending, so you can begin deciding what you're spending too much on, and where you can cut painlessly.

The other thing about keeping a spending diary is that simply by monitoring, you'll find yourself changing your spending. Perhaps you'll start noticing that you're spending $3.50 a pop on fancy coffee drinks three times a day at work. Maybe you'll decide you're genuinely getting $11.50 worth of pleasure from that each day, or maybe you'll decide that you'd be happy enough to drink the company coffee for free and use that $250 a month for something else.

Perhaps your calculations will even lead you to healthier habits. Is that daily pastry or pack of cigarettes helping you in your goals of financial and physical health? Could that gas and electric bill be cut by changing your thermostat or investing in fluorescent lights? Are you getting your money's worth from your cable TV subscription, or could that time and money be better spent?

The answer to these questions may primarily be subjective, but if you want to start planning and saving wisely, it will require data and analysis. So get your Palm Pilot (or even better, an inexpensive pocket-sized notebook) and start taking notes. Make totals by category and after a day, a week, and a month, see where your money is going. We guarantee that this alone will change the way you spend money . . . and what you learn will be valuable data for exercises you'll want to run over the coming weeks.

Many estates are spent in the getting,
Since women for tea forsook spinning
and knitting,
And men for punch forsook hewing and splitting.

It can pay to do the work yourself, even when it comes to caring for your children.

Consider something as mundane as diapers. According to sources like *Mothering Magazine* and Ecomall.com, the cost of putting one child through disposable diapers (assuming two solid years of wearing diapers) is more than $2000, just for purchasing the diapers. Add to that a couple hundred dollars for the cost of the extra garbage, as well.

If you have a baby, or are considering having one, then consider the cloth diaper route. They're healthier, more natural for your baby, healthier for the earth, and the cost is a lot less, even if you use a diaper service.

The cost of doing it yourself will run you about $500-$1000 over the course of the diaper-wearing years. When adding an extra couple of loads to your weekly schedule, consider this: some baby experts argue that when all is said and done, laundering your own cloth diapers *saves* time, and that saved time is actually saved money. If you were using disposables, you would have to go to the store on a regular basis, load and unload the diapers. That kind of time several times a week adds up to far more work than simply rinsing, washing, and drying the extra laundry.

If you use a diaper service, you've saved more time, although less money. The effort's about as hard as teaching yourself to use a recycling bin: dump the dirty diapers into a lined bin. The service delivers new, freshly laundered diapers each week at a cost of around twelve dollars, depending on your area. Total cost over those first couple of years is still usually less than using paper diapers (and better for the world as well).

To save many-a penny, do it yourself.

❦

*'Tis true there is much to be done, and
perhaps you are weak-handed, but stick to
it steadily; and you will see great effects, for
constant dripping wears away stones.*

Speaking of constant dripping, you should look at ways you can save money by eliminating waste. For example, a fast-dripping faucet can cost you a lot of money over time, particularly if it's a hot-water faucet.

Think about conserving and economizing with your home utilities and you're bound to save extra money. Here are a few small ways to get you started:

- Turn the water faucet off while shaving, washing your face, or brushing your teeth. You'll save gallons of water (and some money in the long run).

- Learn to tolerate a wider range of temperature. It takes about two weeks for your body to get acclimated to cold or heat, but if you can let yourself be borderline uncomfortable, your body will adjust. You'll be able to put aside hundreds of dollars from energy savings. Wear sweatpants and a sweater in winter and you can keep your heat well below 68 degrees F. If you can get by with open windows and fans instead of air conditioning in summer—most people did just fine in generations past—you'll conserve resources for our future and cut your electric bills.

- Make sure your refrigerator always runs between 38 and 42 degrees, and your freezer between 0 and 5 degrees. Any cooler on either wastes loads of energy; any warmer and your food will go bad too fast. If your freezer is mostly empty, fill it with frozen orange juice, cartons of milk, or simply bags of ice cubes. It takes less energy to keep solid masses frozen than to keep an empty freezer cold.

- Switch to fluorescent lights. They last forever, and you can keep six going for the price of one of the old-fashioned incandescents. Or better yet, switch to energy-efficient fluorescent light bulbs, which are good for the environment and cost effective. And don't forget to turn thelights off when you leave the room. (Yes, even fluorescents.)

- Put your washing machine cycle on any temperature for the wash cycle, but only on cold for the rinse cycle. Rinsing in cold doesn't affect the cleaning process, and this will save money on your hot-water costs.

- When possible, use a microwave to cook. It uses about one-third of the energy of cooking in a conventional oven.

Make a game of saving energy. Dig out your old utility bills and see how much you can lower them. Make a goal and if you meet it, go out for a modest victory treat . . . and put the rest of your savings into your bank account.

At a great pennyworth pause a while: perhaps the cheapness is apparent only, and not real; or the bargain, by straightening thee in thy business, may do thee more harm than good.

The Sunday paper comes every week with page after page of coupons, promising to take dollars and cents off your grocery bill. On the surface, this seems like a great thing. You spend time clipping them, sorting them, and putting them in place for your next trip to the store; it feels like your budget cogs are all in working order and you're heading on your path to your financial goal.

There are a couple of problems with this weekly habit. "What?" you say. "What could be the problems with clipping coupons?" Well, the truth is that no one ever got rich using grocery store coupons. A few pennies—or even a few dollars—each week rarely add up when you factor in the time it takes you to hunt and clip. It becomes even less cost-effective if you blow more gas and time going from store to store for the "savings" at each. Also, using manufacturer coupons can sometimes lead you to spend more than you would normally. Consider this hypothetical: Tide places a coupon for $2 off their 64-load liquid detergent. If this particular Tide bottle normally sells for $9, it sounds like a great deal. But store brands often run much cheaper, with or without the coupon, so you may end up spending more with coupons if you aren't careful.

You have to factor these things in when you evaluate any "money-saving" activity. Are you saving enough money to make it worth the time you're spending? If you spend half an hour clipping and organizing, are you saving what you'd make if you spent that half hour working your job? Or are you being penny wise and dollar foolish?

Learning is to the studious, and riches to the careful, as well as power to the bold, and Heaven to the virtuous.

You can be one who carefully accumulates riches while helping to give the studious a chance to learn. Benjamin Franklin was a firm believer in supporting your community. You can get a good feeling knowing you've helped someone else while also strengthening your financial situation.

- Have you ever considered using a teaching hospital for your medical care? Teaching hospitals are considerably less expensive than private medical practices. While you're getting medical treatment at a lower price from a medical student, the doctors-in-training are learning valuable lessons and perfecting their skills to take care of others.

- There are also dental schools and optometry schools that specialize in training dentists and eye doctors. All the dental services you'd receive anywhere else are available at a dental school and often, state-of-the-art equipment and new techniques are available at these schools. Call the university in your area and ask if they have a dental school and if services are cheaper there. Or check online for the dental school nearest to you.

- If you have your hair cut at a cosmetology school, you'll get a fabulous 'do along with a much lower bill. You'll also be supporting the training of the cosmetology student.

- Finally, if you want to do good while relieving your survivors of a hefty expense at an emotionally vulnerable time, consider willing your body to science. It's the last gift you can give to others and could save lives. A small environmental bonus is that you won't contribute to the toxic embalming fluids released into the earth or the cremation smoke polluting the air.

What maintains one vice
would bring up two children.

Hobbies and interests are often great things, especially ones that get you to exercise your mind and body, but only if you can effectively budget your time and money.

Some things to think about when you're considering pursuing a leisure-time activity: What is the bare minimum you have to spend to begin? It's easy, out of ignorance and enthusiasm, to buy out the store when you get excited but, for example, barebones camping requires not much more than an inexpensive tent, basic bedding (or even some blankets from home), a few pieces of kitchenware, some inexpensive food and water, and a box of matches. With these things, you can have a profoundly satisfying experience in the woods. Yet, few new campers stop there. Without significantly enhancing the experience, they can spend thousands of dollars on everything from camping chairs to camping espresso makers.

That's true of every sport and hobby: there's an inexpensive way to begin, and an expensive way to begin. Start cheap and find the joys in that, and promise you won't start adding things until you absolutely have to, after having wrung your money's worth out of the original modest investment. Start out with a second-hand bike or a modest pair of running shoes instead of top-of-the-line exercise equipment and a health club membership. If you decide you enjoy the activity and are in it for the long haul, you'll have plenty of time to pursue it and stay within your budget. And if you get bored with an activity and go on to something else, you won't be stuck with thousands of dollars worth of unused photographic equipment, exercise devices, pottery wheels, fishing equipment, etc., gathering dust in a back closet somewhere.

SECTION 7

THRIFT THROUGH SMART SAVINGS

A man may, if he knows not how to save
as he gets, keep his nose all his life to the
grindstone, and die not worth a groat at last.

D o you want an easy investment program that can guarantee returns of hundreds of dollars a year? It's simple—use storage space around your house and apartment and invest your food budget with an eye to the future.

As mentioned, clipping coupons is only rarely worth the time it takes to track them down and organize them. Instead, invest in what we call food futures. Here's how it works: Wherever you shop, look for substantial bargains on expensive things with long shelf lives. They should be non-refrigerated things you normally use or you'll risk losing money if they turn out to be no good. When you find an extraordinary bargain—say laundry detergent or canned coffee at several dollars off—check the "sell-by" date. If it's a long time into the future, figure out how much you would realistically use before that date.

Let's say, for example, that you'd normally use ten large cans of your regular brand of coffee by the freshness date. If the normal price is $9.98 and you can find it on sale for $3.99, buying ten cans, storing them under a bed, and using them as you need them will save you nearly $60 (and more if the retail price goes up in the future, as it often does.) If you can make similar smart purchases on twenty different items a year, and make sure you use the products in time, you can save a bundle. Knowing that you will be saving money, if you need to, you can take a loan from your savings for your "food future" investment and then repay it from future food savings.

When you are considering investing in foods, note that refrigerated items and foods with short shelf dates make poor investments. People who live in earthquake country should also be aware of the risks of buying foods like pickles or peanut butter, which come in glass jars. If an earthquake does occur, it could wipe out your entire savings.

༄

A fat kitchen makes a lean will.

Let's look at a major area where we spend money: food. Do you know how much you spend on food from restaurants, especially fast-food places? According to marketing polls, each American—man, woman, and child—eats out *an average of 140 meals each year,* spending well over a thousand dollars per person. That's *average*—many people eat out more than that, and spend a lot more than that. If you've got a family of four, your savings for more important things could be being discarded like a trayful of used fast-food wrappers.

The worst part of eating large quantities of fast food is not merely that it's a drain on your resources. The worst part is that it's not healthy. Meals are not balanced, they are dripping with bad fat and unnecessary calories, and they perpetuate a taste for more of the same.

The thing is, you're not really saving time and trouble. How much longer does it take to make something healthy than drive to a burger place? Think of ways you can pocket your own money instead of investing in a fast-food conglomerate. Start retraining yourself and your family to enjoy simple, healthy meals in small to modest portions. Start training everybody in the family to prepare good food so the burden and the pleasure of preparing good food is shared. Many kids love to cook for the family, and with a little supervision should be able to handle simple cookbook instructions by the time they are in elementary school. And making pizza with family and friends can be a lot of fun.

"Fast food" usually means a burger and fries. Why not make your "fast food" meals easy to eat and easy to prepare sandwiches, carrots, apples, raisins, etc.—they are tasty, and inexpensive. If that's too much trouble for a groggy, busy morning, make sandwiches the night before—or even the weekend before—and put them in the refrigerator or freeze them. Your kids can make their own sandwiches together on Sunday night.

⚜

Waste not, want not.

If you've never been to a landfill, it's worth a field trip. Truck after truck pulls up and dumps its load. Look down and see what's there—plenty of plastic packaging, wasted food, perfectly good furniture, computers, bicycles, lamps, clothes, lumber, toys, home furnishings. The list goes on and on.

We live in a very wasteful culture. It is our worst, most wasteful habits that cost us so much. It's ironic, for example, that much of our garbage consists of plastic bags, which we toss into a larger plastic bag that we've bought just to help us throw the smaller bags away. We waste so much food, either by throwing it away, or eating to the point of obesity, while millions of people all over the planet go hungry. We buy replacements for everything from furniture to cars to replace items that are perfectly serviceable. We drive to a health club for exercise, when we could get better, cheaper, healthier, and less polluting exercise by walking or biking on our errands. We pay money directly, or through taxes to have our leaves and lawn clippings carried away, and then pay money for fertilizer made from composted leaves and lawn clippings.

Every bit of waste, large or small, is the same as tossing handfuls of money into the street. Save your wealth by reusing, recycling, and conserving.

You may think, perhaps that a little tea, or
a little punch now and then, diet a little
more costly, clothes a little finer, and a little
entertainment now and then, can be no
great matter; but remember, many
a little makes a mickle.

Going to the grocery store without a plan of action is not a good idea. It leads to impulse buying, and that's a real bank account killer. The two most important rules when following a grocery budget are: make a list and stick to it.

Know where your money is going and you will be able to make smart choices.

When you're thinking about stocking up the kitchen, plan your meals. Know, in a general sense, what you'll eat for your three meals a day. Try planning out a week's worth of meals: Simplify the number of options you give yourself. For example, all breakfasts for the week will be toast, cereal, or eggs. All lunches will be either a salad or a sandwich. Think about the fixings you'd like and add these to your shopping list. For dinners, set your menu for the week. Monday night is pasta. Tuesday is rice with beans. Wednesday is quiche. Thursday is oriental stir fry. Friday is low-fat pizza. Saturday will be chicken, beans, and potatoes. Sunday night is for leftovers. Try eating only fresh fruits or vegetables for snacks.

Skip the money-eating, expensive brand names and go for value instead. Know what you'll have available for snacks, and be sure to consume fresh produce before it goes bad. If you decide on a green leaf salad for lunch three times a week, you may have to drop by the store mid-week and pick up a fresh head of lettuce, because purchasing two heads at once will often leave you with one wilted or rotten head.

Consider this your challenge for the week: make your list; check it twice; make sure it only has what you will need; and stick to it! Don't wander around the aisles of the supermarket and buy that extra bag of chips. First and foremost, eat *before* you shop. Shopping when you're hungry will guarantee a bigger grocery bill.

> *Beware of little expenses;*
> *a small leak will sink a great ship.*

Another way to save is with your water heater. It's estimated that a good 20 percent or more of the energy you use in your home goes into heating water. Even if you have an energy-efficient water heater, it still uses a lot of energy to keep you warm in the bath and to clean your dishes.

If you have an older water heater, and you can afford to spend the money, you may want to consider purchasing a solar-heated or energy-efficient water heating system. These can cost between several hundred to several thousand dollars for the heating units, pumps, solar collector, and cost of installation. While in the long run, these may save the most money and natural resources, most of us can't afford that kind of investment.

An alternative to these energy-efficient systems is running low-cost water-saving fixtures. The first place to start is at the faucet. A faucet that is in good order can pump between three and five gallons a minute. Check the seals on your faucet and make sure there are no leaks. Then pick up low water-flow aerators for your faucets. They run less than a few dollars a piece. Aerators mix water with air so you're not using quite as much water while still maintaining the water pressure you need to shower or clean dishes. These aerators can decrease the amount of water you use by 50 percent, or sometimes even more. Also consider buying a low-flow showerhead. A low-flow showerhead releases just two-and-a-half gallons every minute, significantly reducing your overall water usage. You'll make up for the small cost of the new showerhead in no time.

Set your hot-water heater to 130 degrees: high enough to kill dangerous bacteria, and low enough to save you bundles in energy. It also works to put your water heater on the "conservation" setting if you have one. For every ten degrees you lower the temperature, you save 6 percent of the energy you would normally use. Finally, consider investing in a water-heater jacket to help reduce the amount of energy lost from the heater itself. The jacket insulates, helping the water retain its heat longer. Jackets cost about twenty dollars, and can save as much as 7 or 8 percent of the energy you've been using.

You call them goods; but if you do not take care, they will prove evils to some of you.

Sometimes it's worth thinking radically, even heretically. For example, "Does your family really need to own more than one car?" Even better, "Could we live without owning a car at all?"

We don't have to tell you that even a small, gas-efficient car is a huge financial drain. Purchase price, insurance, depreciation, repairs, fuel, and maintenance, can cost between $200,000 to $500,000 over a lifetime. Americans spend more on cars than they do on food—in fact more than they do for any other single expense besides housing. In America, there are more licensed vehicles than there are drivers. Consider the waste and consider the effect having several vehicles has on your ability to save.

Think seriously about the possibility of relocating to biking range of your family's schools, activities, and work. For example. if you moved close to your work, children's school, and stores, and lived in a place with good public transportation, you could easily afford to rent cars for vacation trips and special occasions, and still invest a bundle in savings. If you do this you will save not only money, but also time.

According to census data, the average worker nationwide spends forty-eight minutes commuting to and from work each day. This is *average* and includes people who work from their homes. Many commuters routinely spend two or more hours driving through rush hour traffic each day. Many parents spend too much of their time driving overscheduled children from one marginally beneficial activity to another. Your time is worth more than that. If you can't cut down your commute, at least carpool or take public transportation so you can use that time more productively.

A child and a fool imagine twenty shillings
and twenty years can never be spent.

How do you teach kids about wise money management? You let them exercise decisions about it early. All kids should get an allowance as early as they can understand the idea of money. There is no better way to teach kids how to handle their money. Here's the consensus of experts on the subject:

- Start early. Kids as young as three understand the idea of money.

- An allowance should be paid weekly, and parents should show that they take it seriously by having exact change to be able to pay on time.

- Allowances should not be linked to behavior or chores. You should not present them as a reward or as a measure of love, but as a matter-of-fact payday, a share of household assets that is your child's share of being part of it. Children should also do chores and eat their beans, but keep those separate issues. Allowances should not be withheld nor used as a stick. They should be treated seriously—not as a "reward" but as a salary, teaching your children to become financially responsible.

- For younger children, we suggest having jars marked "long-term savings," "short-term savings" (used like a checking account so they're not carrying large amounts of money around), "spending," and "charity." Guiding your children to allocate some to each jar teaches them how to budget and how to think about others in greater need than themselves. Putting a picture of something they're saving for on their long-term savings jar will help enforce the concept of a savings account.

- Once you've given the allowance, it is not your responsibility to tell them what to do with it (unless, of course, they're spending it on destructive or illegal material). Share with them your values on using money wisely, but let them make their own decisions on how to spend their allowance. Whether they choose to spend it wisely or blow it, it doesn't matter—over time, they're learning consequences and rewards from the experience.

- Although children should be expected to clean up their own messes and do some chores as part of their membership in the family, you may want to consider allowing them to do out-of-the-ordinary chores for additional money.

When the well's dry,
they know the worth of water.

Saving money can be done in simple ways—inside the house and outside of it.

Take your lawn, for example. Most of us must water our grass in order to keep it green. If you limit watering time to the mornings, before the sun has gotten hot, you will save water as less will evaporate before it saturates the soil.

Most grasses are best cut to a two-to-three inch level, not any shorter. During the dry season, leave your grass clippings on the lawn. They help hold in extra moisture, and turn into plant nutrients as they decay.

Outdoor savings can come with a little foresight and investment. Have you considered replanting your property with plants that are native, weather-tolerant and, therefore, require little or no maintenance? With a little research, you can find out exactly which plants will grow best in various parts of your yard and how different species can complement each other. You can cut your water usage in half and save on fertilizer and replantings.

> *'Tis easier to build two chimneys*
> *than to keep one in fuel.*

Fuel is expensive now, as it was in Franklin's time; it's easy to lose a lot of money if you don't keep this in mind around the house. Well-planned and inexpensive home improvements are a great way to save on energy costs.

A well-insulated home means lower energy bills. If you can afford to re-insulate your house, or add an attic, by all means, do so. The energy you will save is worth the building expense, and the value of your house will also increase. If you need to increase the insulation that already exists, the energy savings should cover the costs in about two years' time. Many people don't have the extra funds to do a large job like this. Fortunately, there are still many affordable ways to help stop heat leaks in your house.

To make your home more energy efficient in a cost-effective way, start with the windows. Windows are the biggest energy wasters in any house. Generally, you won't find it cost effective to replace all the windows in your house for better energy-saving ones. Try weather stripping around the seals of doors and windows. This will help hold in some of the air in your house and should improve energy costs. Weather-stripping products are cheap and easy to install. Within a short time, you'll be leaking a lot less heat.

The second step is to invest in a new thermostat for your heating or cooling system. Upper-end thermostats have timers and can allow you to heat or cool only the sections of your house that need it, while closing off other parts. These cost about $100 and will pay for themselves in energy savings quickly. These are a worthwhile investment. It's been estimated that a new, good thermostat can save up to 35 percent of your annual heating or cooling bill.

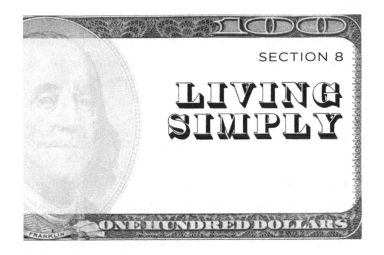

SECTION 8

LIVING SIMPLY

Silks and satins, scarlet and velvets, put out the kitchen fire. These are not the necessaries of life; they can scarcely be called the conveniences, and yet, only because they look pretty, how many want to have them! The artificial wants of mankind thus become more numerous than the natural; and, for one poor person, there are a hundred indigent.

A Jewish sage named Moses Maimonides made a similar comment more than five centuries before Franklin. He said, "The more necessary a thing is for living beings, the more easily it is found and the cheaper it is. The less necessary it is, the rarer and dearer it is. For example, air, water, and food are indispensable to man. . . . No intelligent person, I think, considers musk, amber, rubies, and emeralds as very necessary for man."

The reality is that we want an awful lot. Blame it on the culture—we have an economic system based on spending irrationally. We are constantly encouraged to buy new things, things, and more things. Television bombards us with commercial messages continuously. According to one study, TV-viewing children are bombarded with more than 360,000 commercial messages before graduating high school. And it's not just TV. Catalogs, websites, store windows, counter displays, billboards, magazine ads, peer pressure, and role models all entice us to consume more than we need. Targeted marketing based on your buying patterns keeps pushing your buy buttons. We suggest paying with cash and not responding to surveys just to make it a little bit harder for the marketers to keep track of your buying habits.

Do you know what your personal triggers are? Do you know why you can be made to feel so dissatisfied with the perfectly good belongings you already have, and why you'd be willing to sacrifice financial security to replace them? When we buy because of these triggers, it's no longer a response to a rational need, it's a compulsive response, or for some, even an addiction! And, as with any addiction, it's easy to deny it, justify it, and even find plausible excuses for it that a hundred enablers around you will applaud and agree with.

You may not think that advertising affects you. Nobody believes they buy things based on television, but what television "sells" is a whole paradigm based on the idea that buying the right products will make you happier and more successful in life. Giving up this particular trigger can save you a great deal of money. One Harvard economist concluded that, all other factors being equal, each hour of television viewed per week reduces the average person's annual savings by $208.

Your triggers for irrational buying might also come from non-advertising sources: a great product review, a friend's recommendation, the force of habit. These can be equally persuasive.

Stop the unnecessary consumerism. Use products until they break or wear out, and then decide whether you need to replace them. Become a happy tightwad, and watch your fortunes grow.

By extravagancies, the genteel are reduced to poverty, and forced to borrow of those whom they formerly despised, but who, through industry and frugality have maintained their standing.

One mistake people make is to plan their spending based on their gross salary before deductions, instead of on what they make after taxes and other work-related expenses. One financial planner suggests an antidote: Multiply the price of anything you're thinking of buying by 1.67 to get your before-tax cost. In other words, a $1,000 big-screen TV would cost $1,666 of your pretax salary. If you're getting paid $40 an hour gross pay, that $1,000 expenditure wouldn't cost you twenty-five hours of work, but more like forty-four.

Likewise, look at the cost of eating out or paying someone to mow your lawn. When multiplied by the after-tax equation, it suddenly starts looking good to do it yourself. You may find yourself happily washing your own car, fixing your own toilet, cooking your own meals. The tax-free savings can be pretty impressive.

A plowman on his legs is higher
than a gentleman on his knees.

If you're unhappy, no matter what the reality, you'll feel like you never have enough money. If you're happy, you can make the most of any situation.

Many people with money are really impoverished, because they aren't happy. Not happy enough to appreciate what they have, they spend extravagantly for the momentary lift it brings. They buy flashy status symbols so they can vicariously feel the joy of other people envying their lives. They put their fortunes in jeopardy and impoverish their lives.

How much better it is to have little money but realize the rich possibilities of life. People who are poor in spirit can travel the world and get nothing; while those who are rich in spirit can vacation in their hometown and have the time of their lives.

To make a million dollars a year and spend a million and a half is a recipe for misery and disaster; to make $20,000 and spend your salary wisely, saving $4,000, can make you feel rich indeed.

Pride is as loud a beggar as want,
and a great deal more saucy.

A nice home. Everybody wants one. Unfortunately, many people use their homes as status symbols of their success, and too many confuse having a nice home with having an expensive one, letting their pride get in the way of good money management. Housing is typically going to be your single largest expense, so it's the one at which you should look most carefully.

Real estate agents like to tell clients to "buy as much house as you can afford." Don't follow their advice. Better advice would be "buy the smallest house you can comfortably live in and pocket the savings." That's because with everything from mortgage payments to insurance to heating and cooling, the smaller house wins the economy race every time.

Buy what thou hast no need of, and ere long thou shalt sell thy necessaries.

How much of the money you spend directly addresses genuine needs—basic food, shelter, protection from the elements?

If we spent money only on the basics, almost everybody but the very poor would have plenty left over. However, we live in a world inundated with advertisements, with a deliberate effort to trick us into mistaking wants for needs, brand-name processed food for real nutrition, expensive, sugared, and carbonated water for liquid nourishment. We live in a world where people are constantly beleaguered with messages that they'll be loved and accepted; that they'll be the person they want to be; that they'll get respect from themselves, their neighbors, and potential sexual partners; if only they'd buy the right products.

A used car, a bus, or a bicycle will get you down the road just as effectively as a "luxury car." Designer clothes will make your life no better than off-brand clothes. A soft drink or brand of ice cream will not make you a better person.

Buy what you need. Live well as you live cheaply. There is no reason to take pride because you own things; take pride in how smart you are as you follow your own path.

When you have bought one fine thing, you must buy ten more, that your appearance may be all of a piece. 'Tis easier to suppress the first desire than to satisfy all that follow it.

Ol' Ben has it right here. Who hasn't had the experience of buying a new piece of furniture and then discovering that it makes the rest of the room look shabby in comparison? Or finding that one new article of clothing spurs a buying binge of other clothes, shoes, and accessories? Or finding that a new tree in the yard throws everything else out of balance?

It's more than just appearances. The same domino effect can be just as true with anything else that involves related components. For example, a new computer monitor can make your old software seem old, a new piece of electronic equipment can make your two-year-old stereo or TV seem outdated, a new woodworking or kitchen tool can spur a craving for other power accessories, and so on.

It won't help in the long run just to suppress your urge to upgrade. It will help if you make saving money your new "fine thing." How can you use frugality as your new prized acquisition, the thing that spurs you toward making other changes? If you start by saving money on your heating and cooling, you may discover that you'll also get inspired to start looking for ways to save money on gasoline and lighting. If you start recycling your food scraps into compost, you're going to start feeling a little "shabby" and will want to plant a vegetable garden to go with it.

Of what use is this pride of appearance, for which so much is risked, so much is suffered? It cannot promote health; or ease pain; it makes no increase of merit in the person, it creates envy, it hastens misfortune.

Is earning and amassing large amounts of money extremely important to you? How much time do you spend focused on how much you have or are earning?

We live in a consumer culture. Brand-name products are everywhere—on the airwaves, billboards, magazines, and newspaper. Clever advertisers keep busy trying to come up with new ways to convince us that we must have these brand-name products to be happy or even to survive. If you didn't know you needed an especially absorbent paper towel before, try watching a few hours of morning TV programming and you'll be scrambling to pick some up on your next supermarket outing. The more money you have, the more "stuff" you can get. This kind of external pressure is what drives many to put their money-earning ability ahead of all other priorities.

Most of us have been guilty, at least once in our lives, of judging someone for what they have or don't have. The belief that "money makes the man (or woman)" is so much a part of our consumer psyche, that the ability to make a lot of money has become an integral societal value. What drives the need to race after the next big deal, or to work eighty-hour weeks in order to make a top management position? Again, it may be time to look more closely at your thoughts and feelings. Are you worried about retirement? Do you have a sibling that you may be trying to best? Do you suffer from depression? Sometimes focusing, almost obsessively, on making money can cover these inner feelings. Take a good look at how you see your work and your ability to earn a living. Question your reasons for wanting to have more than you do. Make a list of the things you consider to be the five most important qualities in becoming a good human being. Does "have lots of money" make the list?

What would you think of that prince, or of that government, who should issue an edict forbidding you to dress like a gentleman or a gentlewoman, on pain of imprisonment or servitude? Would you not say, that you are free, have a right to dress as you please, and that such an edict would be a breach of your privileges, and such a government tyrannical? And yet you are about to put yourself under that tyranny when you run in debt for such dress!

Keeping up with the Joneses has become a cliché, but it's an easy trap to fall into. Think for a minute about your priorities. You're a good person. You value the same things most people do: honesty, love, trust, freedom—the list goes on. However, we've all been guilty of trying to impress others. When you walk into a store, and you spy the latest in stereo equipment, how often have you coveted it? Can you honestly say you wanted it because you needed it, or was it because it was simply a cool thing to have? Perhaps your good friend, your brother, or co-worker would be wowed by your "new toy." Or maybe it wasn't any one person you wanted to impress, but that it simply felt good to think about being the kind of person who would own a gadget like that.

There's nothing wrong with being in that place; we all have been. Buying the latest fashion, or leasing a red convertible can give you a super rush. You'll have something to show off and talk about. But if you've spent money on a new item that you really can't afford—either if you don't have enough money, or if it takes money away from your savings goals—the excitement will be fleeting and temporary. The latest fashion is always quickly replaced with something newer. Most of us can't continue to "keep up" by purchasing again and again. And what if you could? Next time you're in the boutique and eyeing a new dress that may fall within your budget, ask yourself why you want it and whether that extra bit of money could be better put to some other use or could serve you better accumulating interest in your savings account. Sleep on it, and see if tomorrow brings a clear answer.

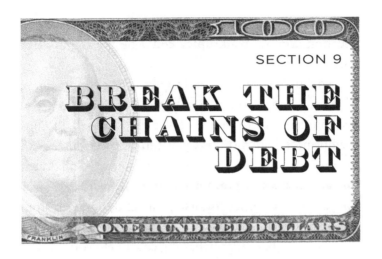

BREAK THE CHAINS OF DEBT

Poverty often deprives a man of all spirit and virtue: 'tis hard for an empty bag to stand upright.

E very year, more than a million people file for personal bankruptcy in the U.S. Most good money advice focuses on keeping you from that point, but what if you're already there? If you put off paying your bills every month, or pay the minimum allowed payment; if you can't pay your bills at all without borrowing money; if you're sick and tired of avoiding collectors that you can't possibly pay, then you're in a bind. It's a difficult situation that has consequences no matter what you do.

But to begin to take responsibility and turn your financial situation around, bankruptcy could be the solution for you.

Two different kinds of bankruptcy exist for individuals: Chapter 7 and Chapter 13. Chapter 7 requires that you petition the court to intervene and help you sell off non-exempt possessions (things you can live without). With the proceeds you pay some or all of your debts off. What this action does is prevent creditors from taking away things you owe money for, like your car or home, or from draining your bank account.

Chapter 13 bankruptcy has the court help you sort out how to pay off your debts within three to five years' time. Property is not sold off in the process, but you must have a large enough income to reach the repayment goals.

To some, this option sounds like a good idea, especially if companies are threatening to take your property. But be aware that if you go the route of bankruptcy, there is fallout that will affect you. For as long as a decade, a bankruptcy filing will show up on your credit report, preventing you from making any big financial purchases where a bank loan may be needed. It also shows up to any potential employers when they run a check on you. It can be a real stumbling block to financial success in the future. Furthermore, bankruptcy cannot help with taxes you owe to the government, or alimony and child support; it can only prevent companies that have given you secured (banks, finance companies) and unsecured (credit card companies) loans from repossessing your property. It would be a very good idea to have a confidential meeting with a consumer credit counselor before considering bankruptcy. Try a non-profit like the NFCC (National Foundation for Credit Counseling).

Always remember: Most companies are usually willing to negotiate with you about payments, if you suck it up and get in touch with them. Try to work out an agreement with them to repay. It's true that late payments are often reported to credit agencies and also show up on your credit report, but they're not as dire a warning to future lending institutions or employers. Bankruptcy is a solution when you have exhausted all others, and one that has many consequences and may affect you negatively for years to come. Work as hard as you can to come up with other solutions first.

Creditors are a superstitious sect, great observers of set days and times.

Finance charges are a real roadblock to savings success. Just about anyone you owe—from department stores to the electric company—will add extra fees to an overdue balance. An overdue balance fee can occur even if you're only a day late; even if your check is literally in the mail, making its way to a payment center. If you often pay late—if you forget to pay bills on time or if you lose bills frequently—saving extra dollars each month may be easier than you think. Here's how:

- Open a bill as soon as it arrives in the mail. This can sometimes be hard if we haven't yet conquered our bad spending habits, but this step is crucial. On the outside of the envelope write the due date so it's easy to see.

- Keep all bills, a checkbook with a register, and a pen together in one place. A plastic Tupperware container works well, as does a folder, or basket.

- As each bill arrives, insert it into a "date due" order. The bills due the soonest should be at the front of the line, on top of the pile.

- Check the box daily and pay any bills at least one week before the due date. Doing so will help you avoid late payment penalties as well as prevent creditors from tagging your credit report for paying late.

~⚬~

*The day comes round before you are aware,
and the demand is made before you are
prepared to satisfy it. Or if you bear your
debt in mind, the term, which at first seemed
so long, will, as it lessens, appear extremely
short. Time will seem to have added wings to
his heels as well as shoulders.*

When borrowing money, follow these few simple rules
and you'll feel like you're keeping your head above the
water:

- First, calculate the amount of money you actually
  need. When you borrow, be sure to borrow that
  exact amount—no more. If you borrow more
  than you need, it becomes harder to repay.

- Secondly, it's important to try and borrow
  money from close family members before
  heading to a financial institution. Why? To
  keep high interest rates and difficult-to-keep
  contractual terms out of the picture. Close
  friends or family may be able to work with a deal
  that allows you to reimburse over time, gives
  you the option of working some of the debt off,

or not paying interest. If you must go to a bank, make sure the arrangements aren't gouging you.

- Stay within your reimbursement means that if you borrow more than you can feasibly pay back within a reasonable amount of time, you'll feel overwhelmed. It's best to try and do with as little as possible so that in a couple of pay periods, you can have your debt paid off. Whatever you do, though, don't keep borrowing from Peter to pay Paul. If you've over borrowed, be up front. Don't cut into your living expenses and find yourself borrowing from another source to pay off the original source. Work out a deal with the first debt and keep paying your bills on time.

※

Those have a short Lent who
owe money to be paid at Easter.

The typical family of four owns more than a dozen credit cards with a total balance of about $6,000. At an average annual compounding interest rate of 17 percent, that means they're paying about $1,000 a year in interest charges alone.

We've said it before and we'll say it again. If you can do nothing else this year to increase your wealth, this is the most important: Pay off your credit card bills and keep them paid off. If possible, cancel the cards, cut them all up (or at least most of them) and dispose of them. They are effective ways to make sure you overspend, that you pay huge, usurious interest rates, and that your money keeps leaking out of your pockets into the coffers of banks that don't need that money as much as you do. Stop being a chump—get rid of those cards.

Since the borrower is a slave to the lender, and the debtor to the creditor, disdain the chain, preserve your freedom; and maintain your independency: be industrious and free; be frugal and free.

When you get credit card bills, does it make your stomach flip upside down? If so, you're not alone. Getting the bill at the end of the month is hard to deal with. Charging things is literally borrowing money, and you are paying for it: not just in interest, either.

One of the best ways to understand, and therefore take control, of your finances is to pay only with cash. Plastic can be debilitating. It's easy to lose track of what you're spending if the money is never actually in your hands at all. It's much easier to impulse buy and spend money on things outside of your budget when all you do is hand over or swipe your card. Stop using it now!

The stress and strain of paying off your credit card, and of not keeping track of your expenditures is not good for you. Your body pays for the extra worry. Your mind gets muddled with worry over how you're going to pay the bill. You suddenly become immobilized and that doesn't do your finances any good. If you're over your limit and can't pay off your credit card bill, or over budget, sit down right now and work out a plan to set it straight. Repay the bill and set your cards aside. Make a promise to yourself that you'll only use cash and stick to your spending budget. You'll find your mind at ease and your life a lot more peaceful. This, in turn, will help you reach your financial goals.

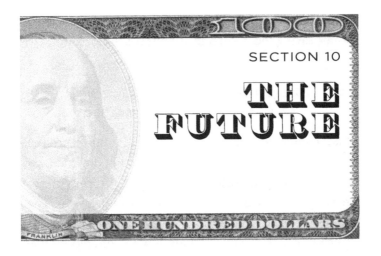

THE FUTURE

One today is worth two tomorrows.

Thinking about tomorrow can be a scary thing, but it can be less scary once you actually start planning for some of the worst cases. How about being laid off or suddenly being incapable of working?

Your job may provide certain kinds of salary insurance against injury, illness, or other emergencies that cause you to lose work. Many companies don't, however, and for those of us who are self-employed, the safety net is more like a web of gossamer. An emergency fund should be part of your savings goal. Some experts say you should have anywhere from three to six months of your annual salary in a savings account "just in case." Another reason to start saving today—it's insurance for tomorrow.

⌘

For age and want, save while you may;
No morning sun lasts a whole day.

Most companies offer some sort of option to help employees save for their retirement, but how do you know if their plan will work out best for your needs? There are a number of resources that can help you. They provide detailed explanations of each long-term savings choice available to you, including plans offered by your company, retirement programs you can start on your own, or a combination of the two. Regardless of what your post-retirement plans may be, it's a good idea to begin thinking about saving for the future. So, what are your options?

A pension is a retirement plan that your company provides for you. Sometimes employers offer a matching funds incentive. In this type of program, the company will contribute the same amount that you contribute to the fund. Another type of plan is a Defined Benefit plan. These pay you a set dollar amount upon retirement—usually a figure that considers the length of time you've been with the company and the amount of money you made over the years. There are also Defined Contribution pension plans. With Defined Contribution Plans, the employee contributes a preset amount each year to a plan like the 401(k), the Simplified Employee Pension (SEP) for small business owners, or the 403(b), which is most often used in tax-exempt organizations. Employee-owned stock ownership and profit sharing plans also fall loosely into this category.

Traditional Individual Retirement Accounts (IRAs) allow one to contribute a certain amount of money each year, tax free. When you withdraw the funds, they're then counted as income and taxed at that time. It's a good way to save on taxes now. There's also a second kind of IRA called the Roth IRA. The Roth IRA works in the same way as a traditional IRA except that you put contributions from your *taxed* income into the fund. When you withdraw, all your earnings are tax free.

There are qualifications to all of these plans that are important to know before deciding which one to pick. Talk to a financial advisor about which one will work best for you.

Since thou art not sure of a minute,
throw not away an hour.

It's amazing the bogeymen that can wake you up in the middle of the night. For example, retirement. If you read articles in books, newspapers, and financial magazines, you'll hear repeatedly that no matter how much you've saved, you're in danger of living your twilight years in a cardboard box. Calm yourself. Fear can motivate you to do things that are not in your best interest and there's a financial motive for investment companies to instill fear in you about the future.

It's true that saving money for retirement—like saving money, in general—is important, but retirement isn't what it used to be. Much of the retirement advice is based on the idea that you want to retire in luxury in your early- to mid-sixties, and then putter idly around the house or play golf or canasta until you die. Today, people are living longer, healthier lives. Many people feel like they're just hitting their stride as they approach their sixties. Many feel that a life of enforced leisure would be hellish, and choose to work well past the age of sixty-five by choice.

Many health experts believe this is better for us anyway. When retirement hits and someone quits working, it can be difficult to adjust. Continuing to have purpose and staying gainfully occupied is key to staying healthy and happy.

With this in mind, then, how does one face retirement? Some suggestions include looking at retirement as a career change. Now, it's true that the Fortune 500 may not be hiring the sixty-plus crowd with no experience in a particular field, but your new work doesn't have to offer the same hours, pay, perks, and stress that your former career did. It simply needs to be something that will keep you occupied and productive, while augmenting your Social Security funds, pension, savings, etc. If it's something that allows you to follow a dream or two, then all the better, but happiness can be found in learning a new skill; in mingling with people; in giving advice to younger people too.

On the other hand, you might have the energy to start something completely new. For example, Harlan Sanders dabbled with a variety of undistinguished jobs throughout his life, but didn't really come into his own until he spent a Social Security check on a fry cooker, a bunch of chickens, and a dozen herbs and spices. This "retiree" experimented until he found the perfect recipe for fried chicken. He franchised it and made a post-retirement fortune as the founder of Kentucky Fried Chicken.

So don't sweat over impossible-to-achieve retirement programs. The key is to save what you can, and vow to keep on living fully, regardless of your age.

ONE LAST THOUGHT

Do not depend too much upon your own industry, and frugality, and prudence, though excellent things; for they may all be blasted, without the blessing of heaven; and, therefore, ask that blessing humbly, and be not uncharitable to those that at present seem to want it, but comfort and help them. Remember, Job suffered, and was afterwards prosperous.

If you're doing well, be humble about it. No one is truly self-made; somewhere along the line, you likely got a boost from a family member, a friend, a trust fund, a scholarship, a teacher, or a tax- and charity-supported institution.

Not everybody is as lucky as you, no matter how modest your riches may be. People were born in the wrong part of the city or the world; perhaps they had terrible parenting, drug addiction, mental illness, or a lack of knowledge, hope, experience, or opportunity. Consider that the average income for a citizen of the world is only $800 per year. There, but for good fortune, go you and I.

Despite America's riches, the average American gives only 3.2 percent of their income to charity. The average American household gives $1,620 to charity each year—about $3 a day, not a lot more than they spend on dry cleaning annually. Ironically, it's the poorest people who give the highest percentage—people making less than $10,000 donated 5.2 percent of their income.

Ben Franklin was a generous man. In his will, he left the cities of Boston and Philadelphia a large chunk of his fortune, with the provision that they use the interest to give loans to needy apprentices (as he once had been), and that they save half the money for 100 years and the other half for 200 years. In 1990, the remaining half of the 2,000 pounds sterling he left was worth $6.5 million.

So be humble, be thankful, and be generous to charity. No matter how much or little you make, you can afford to dig in your pocket to help. No matter how poor you are, there is somebody much worse off than you. Share your wealth with others and you yourself will be blessed many times over.

Reader, if thou wilt do the same,
thy profit will be as great as mine.

APPENDIX

The Way to Wealth
By Richard Saunders
(aka Benjamin Franklin)

Courteous Reader,

I have heard, that nothing gives an author so great pleasure as to find his works respectfully quoted by other learned authors. This pleasure I have seldom enjoyed; for though I have been, if I may say it without vanity, an eminent author of almanacs annually now a full quarter of a century, my brother authors in the same way, for what reason I know not, have ever been very sparing in their applauses, and no other author has taken the least notice of me, so that did not my writings produce me some solid pudding, the great deficiency of praise would have quite discouraged me.

I concluded at length, that the people were the best judges of my merit; for they buy my works; and besides, in my rambles, where I am not personally known, I have frequently heard one or another of my adages repeated with "as Poor Richard says" at the end on't; this gave me some satisfaction, as it showed not only that my instructions were regarded, but discovered likewise some respect for my authority; and I own, that to encourage the practice of remembering and repeating those wise sentences, I have sometimes quoted myself with great gravity.

Judge, then, how much I must have been gratified by an incident I am going to relate, to you. I stopped my horse lately, where a great number of people were collected at an auction of merchants' goods. The hour of the sale not being come, they were conversing on the badness of the times; and one of the company called to a plain, clean, old man, with white locks, "Pray, Father Abraham, what think you of the times? Will not these heavy taxes quite ruin the country? How shall we ever be able to pay them? What would you advise us to?" Father Abraham stood up, and replied, "If you would have my advice, I'll give it you in short; for *a word to the wise is enough, and many words won't fill a bushel,* as Poor Richard says." They joined in desiring him to speak his mind, and gathering round him, he proceeded as follows.

"Friends," says he, "and neighbors, the taxes are indeed very heavy, and, if those laid on by the government were the only ones we had to pay, we might more easily discharge them; but we have many others, and much more grievous to some of us. We are taxed twice as much by our idleness, three times as much by our pride, and four times as much by our folly; and from these taxes the commissioners cannot ease or deliver us, by allowing an abatement. However, let us hearken to good advice, and something may be done for us; *God helps them that help themselves,* as Poor Richard says, in his Almanac of 1733.

"It would be thought a hard government, that should tax its people one-tenth part of their time, to be employed in its service; but idleness taxes many of us much more; sloth, by bringing on diseases, absolutely shortens life. *Sloth, like rust, consumes faster than labor wears; while the used key is always bright,* as Poor Richard says. *But dost thou love life, then do not squander time, for that is the stuff life is made of,* as Poor Richard says. How much more than is necessary do we spend in sleep, forgetting, that *The sleeping fox catches no poultry,* and that *There will be sleeping enough in the grave,* as Poor Richard says.

"*If time be of all things the most precious, wasting time must be,* as Poor Richard says, *the greatest prodigality;* since, as he elsewhere tells us, *Lost time is never found again; and what we call time enough, always proves little enough.* Let us then up and be doing, and doing to the purpose; so by diligence shall we do more with less perplexity. *Sloth makes all things difficult, but industry all easy;* and *He that riseth late must trot all day, and shall scarce overtake his business at night;* while *Laziness travels so slowly, that Poverty soon overtakes him. Drive thy business, let not that drive thee;* and *Early to bed, and early to rise, makes a man healthy, wealthy, and wise,* as Poor Richard says.

"So what signifies wishing and hoping for better times? We may make these times better, if we bestir ourselves. *Industry need not wish, and he that lives upon hopes will die fasting. There are no gains without pains; then help, hands, for I have no lands;* or, if I have, they are smartly taxed. *He that hath a trade hath an estate; and he that hath a calling, hath an office of profit and honor,* as Poor Richard says; but then the trade must be worked at, and the calling followed, or neither the estate nor the office will enable us to pay our taxes. If we are industrious, we shall never starve; for, *At the working man's house hunger looks in, but dares not enter.* Nor will the bailiff or the constable enter, for *Industry pays debts, while despair increaseth them.* What though you have found no treasure, nor has any rich relation left you a legacy, *Diligence is the mother of good luck, and God gives all things to industry. Then plough deep while sluggards sleep, and you shall have corn to sell and to keep.* Work while it is called to-day, for you know not how much you may be hindered to-morrow, which makes Poor Richard say, *one today is worth two tomorrows,* and farther, *have you somewhat to do tomorrow, do it today.* If you were a servant, would you not be ashamed that a good master should catch you idle? Are you then your own master, *be ashamed to catch yourself idle,* as Poor Dick says. When there is so much to be done for yourself, your family, your country, and your gracious king, be up by peep of day; *let not the sun look down and say, inglorious here he lies.* Handle your tools without mittens; remember, that *the cat in gloves catches no mice,* as Poor Richard says. 'Tis true there is much to be done, and perhaps you are weak-handed, but stick to it steadily; and you will see great effects, for *constant dropping wears away stones;* and *by diligence and patience the mouse ate in two the cable; and little strokes fell great oaks,* as Poor Richard says in his Almanac, the year I cannot just now remember.

"Methinks I hear some of you say, 'Must a man afford himself no leisure?' I will tell thee, my friend, what Poor Richard says, *employ thy time well, if thou meanest to gain leisure; and, since thou art not sure of a minute, throw not away an hour.* Leisure is time for doing something useful; this leisure the diligent man will obtain, but the lazy man never; so that, as Poor Richard says, *a life of leisure and a life of laziness are two things.* Do you imagine that sloth will afford you more comfort than labor? No, for as Poor Richard says, *trouble springs from idleness, and grievous toil from needless ease. Many, without labor, would live by their wits only, but they break for want of stock.* Whereas industry gives comfort, and plenty, and respect; *fly pleasures, and they'll follow you. The diligent spinner has a large shift; and now I have a sheep and a cow, everybody bids me good morrow;* all of which is well said by Poor Richard.

"But with our industry we must likewise be steady, settled, and careful, and oversee our own affairs with our own eyes, and not trust too much to others; for, as Poor Richard says:

> I never saw an oft-removed tree,
> Nor yet an oft-removed family,
> That throve so well as those that settled be.

And again, *three removes is as bad as a fire;* and again, *keep thy shop, and thy shop will keep thee;* and again, *if you would have your business done, go; if not, send.* And again,

> He that by the plow would thrive,
> Himself must either hold or drive.

And again, *the eye of the master will do more work than both his hands;* and again, *want of care does us more damage than want of knowledge;* and again, *not to oversee workmen is to leave them your purse open.* Trusting too much to others' care is the ruin of many; for as the Almanac says, *In the affairs of this world men are saved, not by faith, but by the want of it;* but a man's own care is profitable; for, saith Poor Dick, *learning is to the studious,* and *riches to the careful,* as well as *power to the bold,* and *heaven to the virtuous,* and, farther, *if you would have a faithful servant, and one that you like, serve yourself.* And again, he adviseth to circumspection and care, even in the smallest matters, because *sometimes a little neglect may breed great mischief;* adding, *for want of a nail the shoe was lost; for want of a shoe the horse was lost; and for want of a horse the rider was lost, being overtaken and slain by the enemy; all for want of care about a horseshoe nail.*

"So much for industry, my friends, and attention to one's own business; but to these we must add frugality if we would make our industry more certainly successful. A man may, if he knows not how to save as he gets, keep his nose all his life to the grindstone, and die not worth a groat at last. *A fat kitchen makes a lean will;* and

> Many estates are spent in the getting,
> Since women for tea forsook spinning and
> knitting,
> And men for punch forsook hewing and
> splitting.

If you would be wealthy, think of saving as well as of getting. The Indies have not made Spain rich, because her outgoes are greater than her incomes.

"Away then with your expensive follies, and you will not then have so much cause to complain of hard times, heavy taxes, and chargeable families; for

> Women and wine, game and deceit,
> Make the wealth small and the want great.

And farther, *What maintains one vice would bring up two children.* You may think, perhaps, that a little tea, or a little punch now and then, diet a little more costly, clothes a little finer, and a little entertainment now and then, can be no great matter; but remember what Poor Richard says, *many a little makes a mickle;* and farther, *Beware of little expenses; a small leak will sink a great ship;* and again, *who dainties love shall beggars prove;* and moreover, *fools make feasts, and wise men eat them.*

"Here you are all got together at this sale of fineries and knick-knacks. You call them goods; but, if you do not take care, they will prove evils to some of you. You expect they will be sold cheap, and perhaps they may for less than they cost; but, if you have no occasion for them, they must be dear to you. Remember what Poor Richard says; *buy what thou hast no need of, and ere long thou shalt sell thy necessaries.* And again, *at a great pennyworth pause a while:* he means, that perhaps the cheapness is apparent only, and not real; or the bargain, by straightening thee in thy business, may do thee more harm than good. For in another place he says, *many have been ruined by buying good pennyworths.* Again, Poor Richard says, *'tis foolish to lay out money in a purchase of repentance;* and yet this folly is practiced every day at vendues, for want of minding the Alamanac. *Wise men,* as Poor Dick says, *learn by others' harms, fools scarcely by their own;* but *felix quem faciunt aliena pericula caustum.* Many a one, for the sake of finery on the back, have gone with a hungry belly and half-starved their families. *Silks and satins, scarlet and velvets, put out the kitchen fire.*

"These are not the necessaries of life; they can scarcely be called the conveniences; and yet, only because they look pretty, how many want to have them! The artificial wants of mankind thus become more numerous than the natural; and, as Poor Dick says, *for one poor person, there are an hundred indigent.* By these, and other extravagances, the genteel are reduced to poverty, and forced to borrow of those whom they formerly despised, but who, through industry and frugality have maintained their standing; in which case it appears plainly, that *a plowman on his legs is higher than a gentleman on his knees,* as Poor Richard says. Perhaps they have a small estate left them, which they knew not the getting of; they think, "Tis day, and will never be night'; that a little to be spent out of so much is not worth minding; *a child and a fool,* as Poor Richard says, *imagine twenty shillings and twenty years can never be spent* but, *always taking out of the meal-tub, and never putting in, soon comes to the bottom;* as Poor Dick says, *when the well's dry, they know the worth of water.* But this they might have known before, if they had taken his advice; *if you would know the value of money, go and try to borrow some; for, he that goes a borrowing goes a sorrowing;* and indeed so does he that lends to such people, when he goes to get it in again. Poor Dick farther advises, and says,

> Fond pride of dress is sure a very curse;
> E'er fancy you consult, consult your purse.

And again, *pride is as loud a beggar as want, and a great deal more saucy.* When you have bought one fine thing, you must buy ten more, that your appearance may be all of a piece; but Poor Dick says, *'tis easier to suppress the first desire, than to satisfy all that follow it.* And 'tis as truly folly for the poor to ape the rich, as for the frog to swell, in order to equal the ox.

> Great estates may venture more,
> But little boats should keep near shore.

'Tis, however, a folly soon punished; for *pride that dines on vanity sups on contempt,* as Poor Richard says. And in yet another place, *pride breakfasted with plenty, dined with poverty, and supped with infamy.* And after all, of what use is this pride of appearance, for which so much is risked, so much is suffered? It cannot promote health, or ease pain; it makes no increase of merit in the person, it creates envy, it hastens misfortune.

> What is a butterfly? At best
> He's but a caterpillar dressed.
> The gaudy fop's his picture just,

as Poor Richard says.

"But what madness must it be to run in debt for these superfluities! We are offered, by the terms of this sale, six months' credit; and that perhaps has induced some of us to attend it, because we cannot spare the ready money, and hope now to be fine without it. But, ah, think what you do when you run in debt; you give to another power over your liberty. If you cannot pay at the time, you will be ashamed to see your creditor; you will be in fear when you speak to him, you will make poor pitiful sneaking excuses, and by degrees come to lose your veracity, and sink into base downright lying; for, as Poor Richard says, *The second vice is lying, the first is running in debt.* And again to the same purpose, *Lying rides upon debt's back.* Whereas a freeborn Englishman ought not to be ashamed or afraid to see or speak to any man living. But poverty often deprives a man of all spirit and virtue: *'tis hard for an empty bag to stand upright,* as Poor Richard truly says.

"What would you think of that prince, or of that government, who should issue an edict forbidding you to dress like a gentleman or gentlewoman, on pain of imprisonment or servitude? Would you not say, that you were free, have a right to dress as you please, and that such an edict would be a breach of your privileges, and such a government tyrannical? And yet you are about to put yourself under such tyranny, when you run in debt for such dress! Your creditor has authority, at his pleasure, to deprive you of your liberty, by confining you in gaol for life, or to sell you for a servant, if you should not be able to pay him! When you have got your bargain, you may, perhaps, think little of payment; but *creditors,* Poor Richard tells us, *have better memories than debtors;* and in another place says, *creditors are a superstitious sect, great observers of set days and times.* The day comes round before you are aware, and the demand is made before you are prepared to satisfy it, or if you bear your debt in mind, the term which at first seemed so long will, as it lessens, appear extremely short. Time will seem to have added wings to his heels as well as shoulders. *Those have a short Lent,* saith Poor Richard, *who owe money to be paid at Easter.* Then since, as he says, *The borrower is a slave to the lender, and the debtor to the creditor,* disdain the chain, preserve your freedom; and maintain your independency: be industrious and free; be frugal and free. At present, perhaps, you may think yourself in thriving circumstances, and that you can bear a little extravagance without injury, but,

> For age and want, save while you may;
> No morning sun lasts a whole day,

as Poor Richard says. Gain may be temporary and uncertain, but ever while you live, expense is constant and certain; and *'tis easier to build two chimneys than to keep one in fuel,* as Poor Richard says. So, *rather go to bed supperless than rise in debt.*

> Get what you can, and what you get hold;
> 'Tis the stone that will turn all your lead
> into gold,

as Poor Richard says. And when you have got the philosopher's stone, sure you will no longer complain of bad times, or the difficulty of paying taxes.

"This doctrine, my friends, is reason and wisdom; but, after all, do not depend too much upon your own industry, and frugality, and prudence, though excellent things; for they may all be blasted, without the blessing of Heaven; and, therefore, ask that blessing humbly, and be not uncharitable to those that at present seem to want it, but comfort and help them. Remember, Job suffered, and was afterwards prosperous.

"And now, to conclude, *experience keeps a dear school, but fools will learn in no other, and scarce in that;* for it is true, *we may give advice, but we cannot give conduct,* as Poor Richard says; however, remember this, *they that won't be counseled, can't be helped,* as Poor Richard says: and farther, that, *if you will not hear reason, she'll surely rap your knuckles."*

Thus the old gentleman ended his harrangue. The people heard it, and approved the doctrine, and immediately practiced the contrary, just as if it had been a common sermon; for the vendue opened, and they began to buy extravagantly, notwithstanding his cautions and their own fear of taxes. I found the good man had thoroughly studied my almanacs, and digested all I had dropped on these topics during the course of five and twenty years. The frequent mention he made must have tired any one else, but my vanity was wonderfully delighted with it, though I was conscious that not a tenth part of the wisdom was my own, which he ascribed to me, but rather the gleanings I had made of the sense of all ages and nations. However, I resolved to be the better for the echo of it; and though I had at first determined to buy stuff for a new coat, I went away resolved to wear my old one a little longer. Reader, if thou wilt do the same, thy profit will be as great as mine. I am, as ever, thine to serve thee,

Richard Saunders
July 7, 1757